Pebble® Plus

T0042169

My Circulatory System

A 4D Book

by Martha E. H. Rustad

Consultant:
Natasha Kasbekar, M.D., Pediatrician
Kids Health Partners, LLC, Skokie, Ill.

PEBBLE
a capstone imprint

This is a Capstone 4D book!

Want fun videos that go with this book?

Just visit www.capstone4d.com

Use this password
blood.00207

Pebble Plus is published by Pebble
1710 Roe Crest Drive, North Mankato, Minnesota 56003
www.capstonepub.com

Library of Congress Cataloging-in-Publication Data
Names: Rustad, Martha E. H. (Martha Elizabeth Hillman), 1975– author.
Title: My circulatory system : a 4D book / by Martha E. H. Rustad.
Description: North Mankato, Minnesota : Pebble, [2019] | Series: Pebble
    Plus. My body systems | Audience: Age 4–8.
Identifiers: LCCN 2018004144 (print) | LCCN 2018004310 (ebook) |
    ISBN 9781977100283 (eBook PDF) | ISBN 9781977100207 (hardcover) |
    ISBN 9781977100245 (pbk.)
Subjects: LCSH: Cardiovascular system—Juvenile literature. | Blood—
    Circulation—Juvenile literature.
Classification: LCC QP103 (ebook) | LCC QP103 .R87 2019 (print) |
    DDC 612.1—dc23
LC record available at https://lccn.loc.gov/2018004144

Editorial Credits
Emily Raij, editor; Charmaine Whitman, designer; Morgan Walters,
media researcher; Laura Manthe, production specialist

Image Credits
iStockphoto: JLBarranco, 11, theboone, 5; Shutterstock: arborelza, 7,
chombosan, 17, imaginarybo, design element throughout, kornnphoto,
15, Lopolo, (girl) Cover, sciencepics, 9, Sladic, 13, Srijaroen, 19, Tetiana
Saienko, (heart) Cover, TinnaPong, 1, wavebreakmedia, 21, yodiyim,
(blood cells) Cover

Printed in the United States   5062

Note to Parents and Teachers

The My Body Systems set supports the national science
standards related to structures and processes. This book
describes and illustrates the circulatory system. The
images support early readers in understanding the text.
The repetition of words and phrases helps early readers
learn new words. This book also introduces early readers
to subject-specific vocabulary words, which are defined
in the Glossary section. Early readers may need assistance
to read some words and to use the Table of Contents,
Glossary, Read More, Internet Sites, Critical Thinking
Questions, and Index sections of the book.

Table of Contents

Blood Works Hard

Ouch! I cut my finger.

I see blood.

Dad cleans my cut.

He puts on a bandage.

I wonder what my blood does.

My circulatory system moves
blood around my body.
My heart, blood vessels, and
blood make up this system.
My heart pumps the blood.

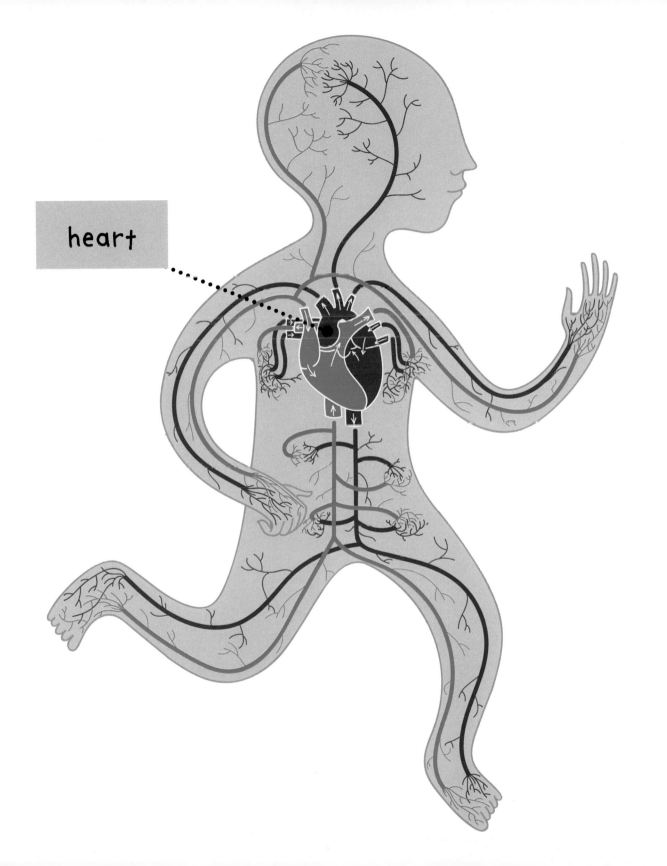

heart

Moving Blood

My blood moves through blood vessels. These tubes carry blood to my heart. They also carry blood away from my heart.

heart

blood vessels

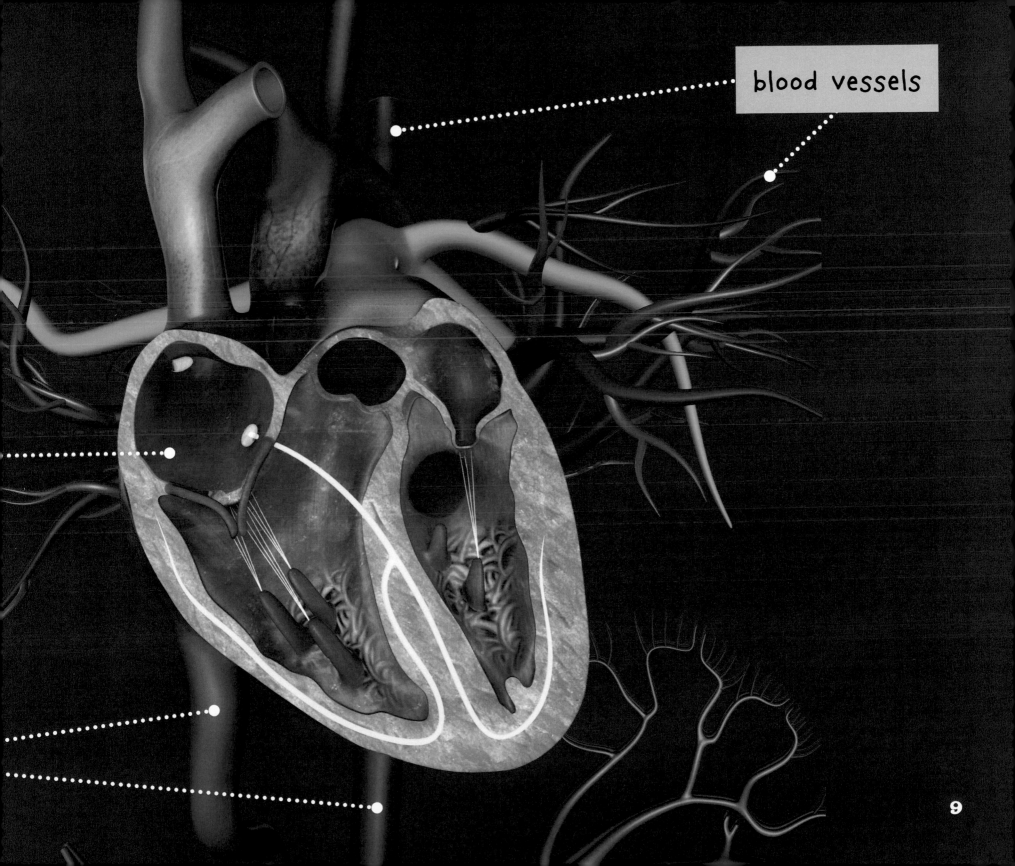

blood vessels

My heart pumps blood to my body. Red blood cells carry oxygen. Oxygen is a gas my body needs. It gives my body energy.

My blood also carries nutrients.

This is food for my body.

Nutrients help my body grow.

Plasma in my blood carries

the nutrients.

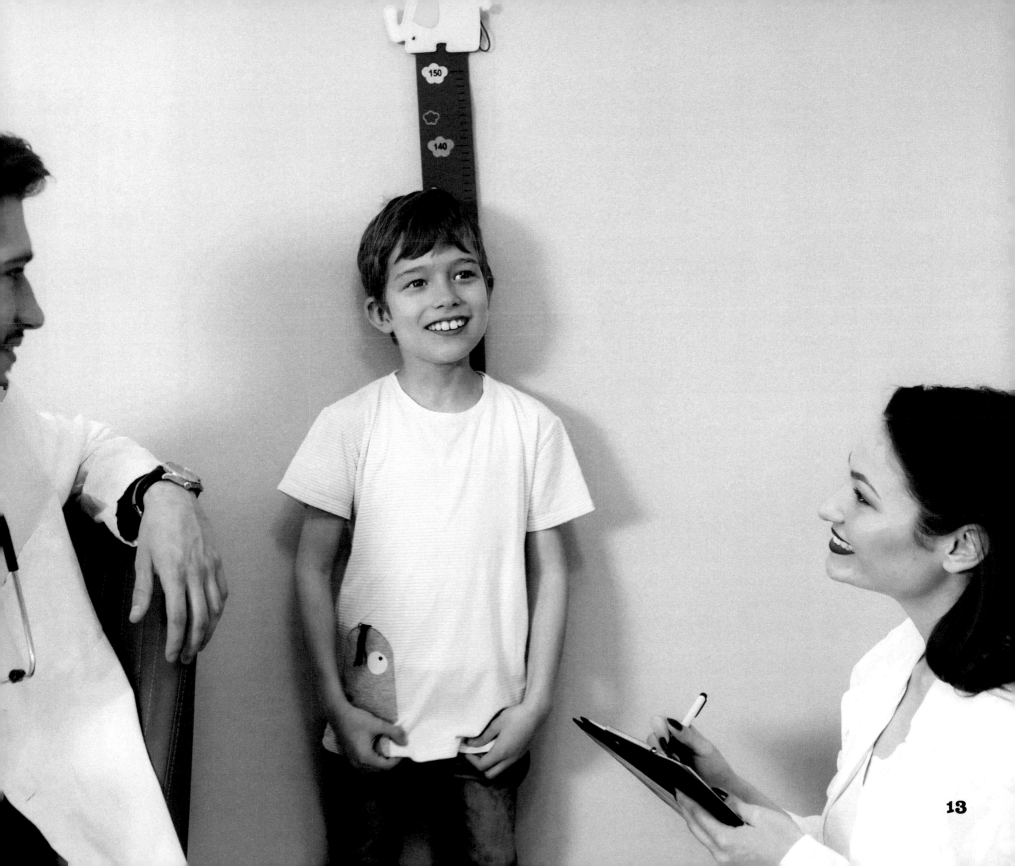

Blood comes back to my heart.

Then blood goes to the lungs

to get oxygen. I take a

deep breath. I am giving

my body oxygen!

My blood also carries waste. Blood moves waste to the lungs and kidneys. Carbon dioxide is one kind of waste. I breathe out this gas.

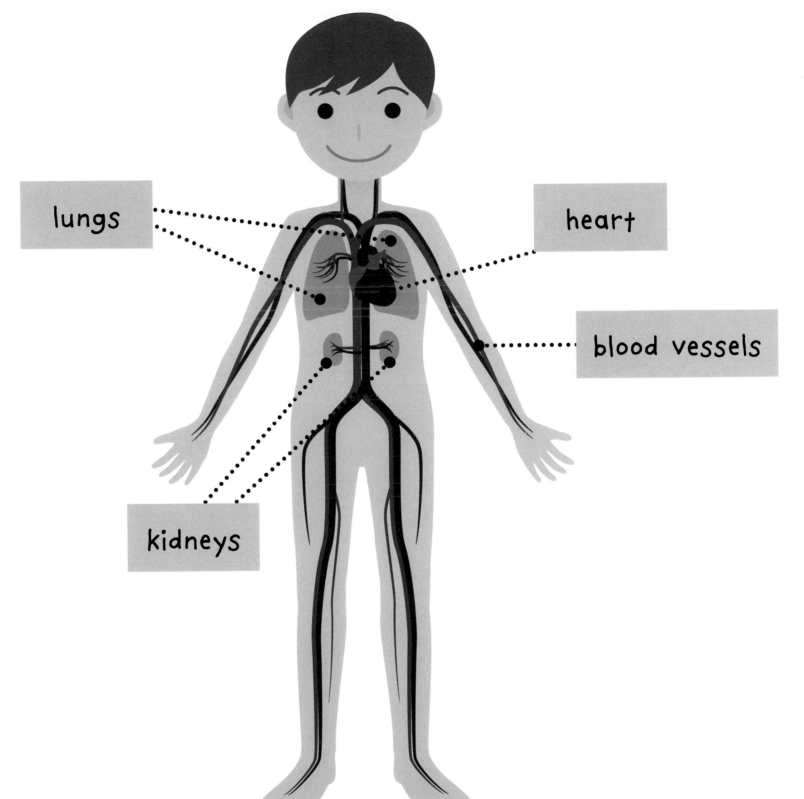

lungs

heart

blood vessels

kidneys

17

Keeping Blood Healthy

My blood works hard for me.

I keep my blood healthy.

I eat good food and

drink water. My blood

carries nutrients to my body.

Exercise makes my heart muscle strong. A healthy heart pumps my blood well. I help my heart and blood so they can help my body.

Glossary

blood vessel—a narrow tube that carries blood through your body

carbon dioxide—a colorless, odorless gas

circulatory system—the system that moves blood throughout your body

energy—the strength to do active things without getting tired

muscle—a tissue in the body that is made of strong fibers; muscles can be tightened or relaxed to make the body move.

nutrient—a part of food, like a vitamin, that is used for growth

oxygen—a colorless gas that people and animals breathe; humans and animals need oxygen to live.

plasma—the liquid part of the blood that carries red blood cells, white blood cells, and platelets

pump—to empty or fill using a pushing motion

Read More

Brett, Flora. *Your Circulatory System Works!* Your Body Systems. North Mankato, Minn.: Capstone Press, 2015.

Halvorson, Karin, M.D. *Inside the Blood.* Super Sandcastle: Super Simple Body. Minneapolis: Abdo, 2016.

Mason, Paul. *Your Hardworking Heart and Spectacular Circulatory System: Find Out How Your Body Works!* Your Brilliant Body! New York: Crabtree, 2016.

Internet Sites

Use FactHound to find Internet sites related to this book.

Visit *www.facthound.com*

Just type in 9781977100207 and go.

Check out projects, games and lots more at
www.capstonekids.com

Critical Thinking Questions

1. What does your blood do?

2. How does blood travel around your body?

3. What is the heart's job?

Index